'. . . Christ . . . leaving you an example for imitation
so that you should follow in his steps'
(1 Peter 2:21)

FOLLOWING JESUS

A Handbook
On Basic Discipleship
For Individual And Group Study

Günter Krallmann

HODDER AND STOUGHTON
LONDON   SYDNEY   AUCKLAND   TORONTO

British Library Cataloguing in Publication Data

Krallmann, Günter
   Following Jesus: a handbook on basic
   discipleship for individual and group
   study. – (Hodder Christian paperbacks).
   1. Christian life
   I. Title
   248.4   BV4501.2

   ISBN 0 340 41588 6

To all Christian brothers and sisters
in southern Africa
who
as true followers of the Lord Jesus
desire to grow into His likeness,
this book
is affectionately dedicated

Table of Contents

Foreword by Floyd McClung

I cannot state too strongly how important I feel this book is.

This book should be put in the hands of every new Christian, every struggling Christian, and should be used by every local church for helping with the discipling process of establishing new Christians in their Christian faith.

Because this book deals with Bible Studies for the new Christian, it is simple enough for a child to understand, but profound enough to challenge a scholar. In a systematic and concise manner, it lays out the foundations of the Christian life.

I would also like to suggest that mature Christians re-evaluate the foundations of their Christian life by studying this book carefully. The importance of building our lives on a solid understanding of the principles of God's Word, and how they are intended to guide our lives, is absolutely essential. It is not enough to study the Bible, book by book, verse by verse, which I believe is extremely important, but it is also important to understand principles topically, and how they apply to our lives.

For example, on page 73, the author deals with the subject of testings and temptations. In this chapter, he tells us how God sometimes tests us as Christians in order to help us grow, learn new lessons, build our character, purify us, humble us, and discipline us. If we do not understand that it is one of God's ways in dealing with us to test us, in order to do these things in our lives, it can bring confusion and frustration. But if we understand that the difficult circumstances we go through are sometimes God's testings in our lives, then it will help us to co-operate with God and not resist what he is doing. It says in Dt 8:2, 'And you shall remember all the way which the Lord your God has led you these forty years in the wilderness, that he might humble you, testing you to know what was in your heart, whether you would keep his commandments or not.'

I have known the author of this book for many years and commend him to you as a man of God who lives what he teaches. He is a man of great compassion, gentleness, wisdom and tender authority. I highly commend him and this wonderful book to you!

Your brother in Christ

Floyd McClung Jr
May 1987

Author's Preface

In the past the extension of the Kingdom of God has often been pursued with the underlying conviction that fulfilling the Great Commission is a matter more of quantity (number of decisions) than of quality (discipleship).

As a consequence, many Christians around the world have never grown out of the stage of spiritual childhood, and in many of the Good Shepherd's flocks there are far more lambs than sheep.

Sadly, a lot of Christians have a rather limited knowledge of the Word, possess little power in prayer, and are confused about God's specific will for their lives. Pastors may discern in their congregations a lack of hunger for the things of God, of zeal to reach the lost, and of leaders who are qualified and willing to help promote the spiritual life and missionary calling of their church.

In the light of such spiritual weakness, would we not do well to *rediscover*, *rethink* and *reapply* the strategy which we find so clearly laid down in the practice and teaching of the Lord Jesus Christ?

Mark 3:14 shows us Jesus calling the Twelve, first to be with Him, before He would then later send them out on ministry. They were to learn and to be moulded in intimate fellowship with Him; they were to be discipled through daily observing His living example and through listening to His teaching. Jesus Himself was His method. Based on the imitation principle, He effectively trained a small core group of simple but committed men to become mature disciples – and thus the leaders for the continuation and extension of the work He had begun.

The abundant fruit of His ministry proved the validity and efficiency of His strategy. Once the eleven Galileans, whom He had diligently trained for three to three and a half years, were empowered by the Holy Spirit, they set the world aflame.

Paul followed his Master in putting the concept of discipleship right at the heart of his missionary strategy (see for instance 2 Timothy 2:2, Acts 14:21–23, 1 Corinthians 11:1). And did not his life and ministry produce absolutely extraordinary results for the furthering of God's Kingdom?

Through the Great Commission (Matthew 28:18–20), the Lord Jesus put all future generations of believers under the mandate to 'train all people groups in discipleship' (verse 19). A closer look at the original text of the passage will reveal that the only imperative verb form used in the Greek is the command to make disciples. Thus, our Lord emphasised His desire that not mere converts but disciples would be made. This implies that ever since the Great Commission was given, the true test of all fruitful evangelistic and missionary endeavour is not how many people are being led to conversion, but how many are actually being trained to become mature disciples.

We cannot improve on the wisdom of God. He has ordained discipleship training as *the* strategy to penetrate effectively the world with the message of His love and salvation. Making disciples, as exemplified by the master discipler, His Son, is still the very best way to see the mandate of the Great Commission fulfilled, and it is the only approach that can expect the confirmation of God's full blessing.

Discipleship training has been and is on the heart of the Lord Jesus. Do we love Him enough to render what was important to Him, also important in our lives and ministries? If we are truly committed to Him as our Lord, the question can no longer be, 'Should I make disciples?' but only, '*How* can I make disciples?'

The vision for this book was born out of a period of ministry in the mountain kingdom of Lesotho in May 1985.

While presenting basic discipleship teaching through a series of messages, the great need for a follow-up manual on biblical discipleship in the Sesotho language became very obvious. However, the need for further study material on this vital subject does not manifest itself amongst Basotho Christians only, but emerges wherever followers of the Lord Jesus Christ truly desire to grow into His likeness and to help others reach their full potential in Him.

This book seeks to provide inspiration, direction and practical help for all those who desire first to follow in the Master's footsteps themselves (see 1 Peter 2:21), and then to train others to do the same. May God grant that *Following Jesus* will contribute towards the realisation of this twofold goal in the lives of many Christians in numerous parts of the world.

I extend my deep gratitude to all those who gave themselves to making this publication possible.

It is my desire to express my great thankfulness and appreciation to the publishers, Hodder & Stoughton, for graciously undertaking the publication of this new edition, thus making the material available to a much wider public.

Special thanks, however, I pass on to my dear wife Ulrike for her loving support, to my son Michael for his prayers, and to my friend Bill Kelley for his steadfast encouragement.

Günter Krallmann
Lionelton, South Africa, April 1987

How to use this handbook

A major purpose of this book is to lead the individual or the group that is using it into a deeper study of the Bible with regard to certain subjects which seem basic to the life-style of a true follower of the Lord Jesus Christ.

Therefore, the approach chosen has not been to readily provide detailed and full answers; rather, the various topics have been treated in outline form, presenting principles with numerous Scripture references and biblical examples. The reader is thus to be directed and encouraged to discover personally the answers needed in the Scriptures themselves. For acquiring a thorough understanding of biblical truth, it seems that the Bereans' approach (Acts 17:11) is still the best, who received the Word of God very eagerly, and then examined the Scriptures continuously to find for themselves confirmation of the truth.

Once the contents of this handbook have been digested through individual or group study as well as applied, then the truths learnt should be passed on to others by using the outlines as a teaching guide.

In this way, not only Paul's pattern for discipleship training will be followed (2 Timothy 2:2), but also the overall object in writing this handbook will be achieved.

'. . . train all the people groups in discipleship . . .'
(Matthew 28:19)

A.

What It Means
To Be A Disciple

(1)

The Lord Jesus Desires Disciples

A. What is a disciple?

1. A disciple is a follower (Mk 2:14, Mk 6:1)*
2. A disciple is a learner (Mt 11:29, Lk 6:40)
   Therefore: A 'disciple' is a Christian who is determined
   to follow Jesus Christ, with the desire to learn from Him
   and to live according to His example. 'Discipleship' is the
   process in the course of which a disciple
   — grows into Christlikeness
   — is being trained into Christlikeness

B. Examples of discipleship-relationships in the Bible

Moses and Joshua	(Nu 11:28)
Elijah and Elisha	(1 Ki 19:19–21)
David and his mighty men	(1 Sa 22:2; 1 Ch 11:10)
John the Baptist and his disciples	(Mk 2:18)
Jesus and the Twelve	
Paul and Silas, Timothy, Titus, etc.	

C. The importance of discipleship

1. During His earthly ministry, Jesus considered
   discipleship of the utmost importance

---

*Pages 118–19 list the abbreviations for the books of the Bible

- besides His 'public' ministry (preaching, teaching, healing, etc.), He engaged Himself in the 'hidden' ministry of training the Twelve
- during the three to three and a half years between His baptism and ascension, He made the training of the twelve disciples a priority

2. Jesus commissioned all following generations to give themselves to the training of disciples (Mt 28:19)
   - Jesus did not formulate this commission as a suggestion or option, but as an absolute obligation
   - Jesus commanded us not to make converts, but **disciples** (He intended fruit that lasts: Jn 15:16)

3. Discipleship is the optimal method to reach our world for God
   - The tremendous missionary impact of the Early Church and Paul's ministry proved the utmost effectiveness of discipleship training for the evangelisation of the world
   - For the growth of the Kingdom of God, quality is more important than quantity:
   A small number of committed disciples, who have been thoroughly trained into Christlikeness, will achieve more for God than a large number of converts who lack spiritual depth
   - The making of disciples is God's chosen strategy to reach this world

D. The value of discipleship training

Converts will be led on to become true disciples
Disciples will grow into Christlikeness
They will experience a most satisfying life in closeness to Jesus
The disciples will reproduce their quality of life in others

Through the making of disciples, the evangelisation of the world will be greatly promoted

If we make disciples, we please God, because we take seriously as well as fulfil His desire and command as expressed in Mt 28:19

For further consideration:

Read 1 Pe 2:21. What does it mean practically, to follow in Jesus' steps?

(2)

The Twofold Purpose of Discipleship Training

A. The first goal of discipleship training: to lead Christians to spiritual maturity

Spiritual maturity does not come about automatically through an increase in age, knowledge or experience. Rather, it is the result of gradual spiritual growth, on the basis of obedience to the conditions of true biblical discipleship

What are some marks of spiritual maturity?
— close fellowship with Jesus (Gal 2:20)
— a solid knowledge of biblical truths
— stability and consistency in a holy walk before God and man
— showing the fruit of the Holy Spirit (Gal 5:22–23)
— a humble willingness to serve others
— fruitfulness in ministry
— a standard of excellence in conduct and working for God

All in all: Christlikeness (1 Jn 2:6; Ro 8:29)

Why must we aim at spiritual maturity?
— growth into maturity in Christ is the level of biblical expectancy for all Christians (Heb 5:12 – 6:1; Col 1:28; Eph 4:14–15; Lk 6:40)
— without maturity, there can be no leadership, which is necessary, however, for the church of Christ to grow as well as to fulfil the Great Commission
— only mature believers will be able effectively to

oppose and defeat the devil and his powers of darkness (Mt 12:29)
— only mature Christians can have a real impact for God on our world today
— it is only the mature disciple who – through his living example – is able to convey the wonderful attributes of Jesus' character to the world

B. The second goal of discipleship training: to lead Christians to spiritual multiplication through reproduction

Jesus, the master discipler, called the Twelve with the very purpose of seeing them reproduce themselves (Mt 4:19; Mk 3:14)
He trained them diligently for three to three and a half years to the point where they were able – with the help of the Holy Spirit – to continue and extend His work on earth (Jn 17:4; Mk 16:15; Ac 1:8)
Spiritual reproduction and multiplication come about when a disciple passes the quality of his life in Christ on to others
Examples of spiritual multiplication through reproduction:
— Jesus discipled the apostles; they trained the early Christians, among them Philip; he led the Ethiopian to Christ; tradition names the latter as the founder of the Christian church in Africa (Mt 28:18–20 and Ac 8:26–39)
— Paul trained Silvanus and Timothy; they were imitated by the Thessalonians; these Christians in turn became an example to those in Macedonia and Achaia (1 Th 1:6–8)
— Aquila and Priscilla became Christians; they spent time with Paul; later, they led Apollos into the deeper

things of God; he became a great help to Christians in Achaia (Ac 18:2–3, 18, 24–8)

It is essential to realise:

Through **evangelism** you make converts, thus adding to the number of born-again believers

Through **discipleship training** you make disciples, thus adding mature reproducers, who in turn multiply the number of born-again believers/disciples manifold

For further consideration:

How do you assess the relevance of discipleship training for seeing lasting fruit (Jn 15:16)?

(3)

The Cost of Being a True Disciple

A. Jesus demanded a high price from those who were going to be His disciples

They had to give absolute priority to Him

He expected them

— to love Him first and foremost (Lk 14:26)
— to deny themselves (Mt 16:24)
— to take up their cross (Mt 16:24)
— to follow Him (Lk 14:27)
— to give up everything they had in order to follow Him (Lk 14:33)

Because Jesus demanded such a high price for discipleship, He challenged everyone to first count the cost (Lk 14:28–32)

Not everybody was willing to pay such a high price

— some had reservations or excused themselves (Lk 9:57–62)
— many disciples of the days of Jesus' early ministry, found it too hard to continue walking with Him (Jn 6:60–6)
— the rich young ruler was not willing to place Jesus first in his life (Mk 10:22)

In view of the high cost of discipleship which Jesus required, it is not surprising that He did not start a mass movement, but recruited 'only' a few who were deeply committed to Him

But these few were enough to later change the world!

B. True discipleship will cost us all we have

Living as a true disciple is not a voluntary extra of some particularly zealous Christians; rather, it is the norm of Christian commitment which Jesus expects from all His followers
True discipleship begins with the realisation and willing acceptance of the fact that Jesus rightfully deserves to be made Lord of our whole life (Jn 13:13, see also Col 1:16–17)
A true disciple is the person who has responded to the radical claims of Christ with a radical commitment to Him
It is important to recognise that the high goals of the Kingdom of God – the goals which the Lord Jesus lived and died for – allow neither shallowness, half-heartedness nor mediocrity on the part of those who follow Him

C. Various biblical requirements for true discipleship can, it seems, be focused into a few basic preconditions

1. Loving Jesus first and foremost
    This includes allowing Him to lead our lives according to His will (obedience)
2. Spiritual hunger
    It implies a real desire to grow spiritually and to be used by God
3. A teachable attitude
    It manifests itself through a willing submission to the authority of God's Word and spiritual leaders whom He has placed over us

4. Faithfulness

Paul indicates that only faithful men fully qualify for discipleship training (2 Ti 2:2; see also Lk 16:10–12)

5. A willingness to sacrifice

To grow into spiritual maturity will demand sacrifices of time, strength, at times relationships, etc.

Are we willing to organise our lives according to the discipleship programme that God intends for us personally, to see us formed into the likeness of His Son?

If we realise that we do not fulfil all these five requirements to the extent desired, let us not be discouraged; but rather, let us take courage by looking at God and His Word: Php 2:13

Our faithful God and loving Father is more than able and willing to help: 2 Co 9:8 and 1 Th 5:23–24

For further consideration:

Define the apostle Paul's discipleship strategy as stated in 2 Ti 2:2

B.

Becoming A Disciple

(4)

The Fatherhood of God

A. The perfect Fatherhood of God

God revealed Himself in various ways through the prophets (Heb 1:1)
Jesus, however, revealed particularly God's Fatherhood (Heb 1:2) (See, for instance, the Sermon on the Mount: Mt 5–7)
God is the originator of all fatherhood (Eph 3:14–15)
As He is love (1 Jn 4:8), perfect (Mt 5:48), and our Father (Mt 6:9), we are privileged to experience His perfectly loving Fatherhood (1 Jn 4:18)

B. Loving purposes of God the Father for mankind

He wishes all mankind to be saved	(1 Ti 2:4)
He longs for men to be His children	(Jer 3:19)
He delights to show love	(Mic 7:18)
He purposes to bless us abundantly	(Jn 10:10)
He wants to take care of all our needs	(1 Pe 5:7)
He desires to set us free from fear	(Jn 14:1)
He is ever so willing to answer prayer	(Isa 65:24, Mt 7:11)
He wants to give man an eternal home	(Jn 14:2–3)

C. God perfectly fulfils the offices of a father

Consider Him as e.g.:

Our protector	(Ps 91; Jn 10:27–9)
Our provider	(Mt 6:26–33)
Our helper	(Ps 10:14)
Our comforter	(2 Co 1:3–4)
Our instructor	(Dt 8:3)
Our counsellor	(Ps 73:24)
Our corrector	(Heb 12:5–11)

D. Expressions of His Fatherly love

He is kind	(Lk 6:35)
He is generous	(Jas 1:5)
He is merciful	(2 Co 1:3)
He is compassionate	(Lk 15:20)
He is gentle	(Hos 11:3–4)
He is patient	(Mt 18:26–7)
He is impartial	(1 Pe 1:17)
He is just	(Rev 15:3)
He is faithful	(2 Ti 2:13)
He is attentive to our needs	(1 Pe 5:7)
He gives rest	(Mt 11:28–9)
He forgives	(1 Jn 1:9)

E. The Father-heart of God is moved by men's actions

We read in the Old Testament, and we see in the life of the Lord Jesus who showed us the Father (Jn 1:18; 14:9) that God's heart is affected by man's response to His Father love

Thus He experiences for example:

disappointment	(Eze 22:30–31)
sorrow	(Jer 8:18; Isa 53:3)
grief	(Gen 6:6; Lk 19:41)
mourning	(Jer 8:21)
compassion	(Mt 9:36)
joy	(Lk 15:22–4)
rejoicing	(Zep 3:17)

F. The Fatherhood of God is foundational to the Christian life

For the plan of redemption	(Gal 4:4–7)
For our adoption as sons	(Ro 8:15; 1 Jn 3:1)
For our access to God	(Eph 2:18)
For receiving the Holy Spirit	(Lk 11:13)
For answered prayer	(Mt 7:11)

For further consideration:

What does Lk 15:11–32 reveal about the Fatherhood of God?

(5)

Sin

A. What is sin?

The original text of the New and Old Testaments uses a variety of expressions to show the nature of sin:

Missing the mark	(Ro 3:23)
Transgression of the law	(1 Jn 3:4)
Lawlessness	(2 Th 2:3)
Trespassing	(1 Ti 2:14)
Iniquity	(Tit 2:14)
Evil	(Ro 1:29)
Wickedness	(Ac 3:26)
Ungodliness	(Ro 1:18)
Disobedience	(Heb 2:2)
Rebellion	(Eze 2:3)
Enmity against God	(Ro 5:10)

B. Some consequences of sin

Guilt	(Ps 51:3–4)
No peace	(Ro 3:17)
Lack of hope	(Eph 2:12)
Spiritual blindness	(2 Co 4:4)
No favour with God	(Jn 3:36)
Separation from God	(Isa 59:1–2)
Spiritual death	(Eph 2:5)
Judgement	(Jn 5:29)

Everlasting punishment   (Mt 25:46)
Unending misery   (Rev 14:11)

C. The destructive power of sin

It entangles	(Heb 12:1)
It hinders	(1 Pe 3:7)
It defiles	(Mk 7:20–3)
It darkens the understanding	(Eph 4:18)
It corrupts	(Tit 1:15)
It enslaves	(Ro 6:17)
It condemns	(Jas 5:12)
It evokes God's wrath	(Jn 3:36)
It causes spiritual death	(Eph 2:1)

D. Why sin is so horrible

It grieves God (Gen 6:5–7)
It hinders His intentions for establishing His Kingdom of light
It supports the kingdom of darkness
It sent the Lord Jesus to the cross
It cost the shedding of His precious blood
It harms the sinner
It affects his fellow-men

E. Everyone is responsible for his own sin

Ro 14:12; Eze 18:20–3; Mt 16:27
We all have sinned (Ro 3:23)
We have preferred selfishness to loving God first and foremost

We have unintelligently misused our God-given abilities
(Notice that Pr 24:9 characterises sin as a foolish undertaking)

F. Jesus died for our sins

He sacrificed His life so that we all can be saved from the guilt, consequences, and power of sin

For further consideration:

Study the apostle Paul's teaching about sin in Ro 6:12–23

(6)

Repentance

A. The first major condition to enter the Kingdom of God: repentance

In order to become a Christian – a child of God as well as a disciple of the Lord Jesus Christ – the first necessary step is to repent:
Mt 3:2
Mt 4:17; Lk 13:5
Mk 6:12
Ac 2:38

B. What is true repentance?

It is a totally new orientation in thinking and doing, a complete turnaround in thought and conduct
1. It implies a change of mind
   There is a new perspective of sin (of its nature, awfulness, and consequences)
2. It implies a change of action
   — a turning to God (Ac 26:20; Lk 15:18)
      (a turning from selfishness to loving God, from disobedience to obedience, from rebellion to submission)
   — a turning away from sin (2 Ch 7:14; Ac 14:15)
      (a determination to hate sin, to forsake all sinful ways once and for all)
   — an offering up of ourselves to God for ownership

C. A few evidences of repentance

Confessing sin in prayer	(Lk 18:13)
Making restitution	(Lk 19:8)
Removing idols	(1 Sa 7:3; Ac 19:19)
Serving God	(1 Th 1:9)
Producing good fruit	(Mt 3:8)
Doing good deeds	(Ac 26:20)

D. Some biblical examples of true repentance

David	(2 Sa 12:13; Ps 51)
The prodigal son	(Lk 15:18–21)
Zacchaeus	(Lk 19:1–10)
Simon Peter	(Mk 14:72; Lk 22:62)

E. It is our duty to repent

We have all sinned	(Ro 3:23)

God has rightful claims on our lives:

— He created us	(Ps 139:13)
— He has kept us	(Ps 121:5–8)
— He has loved us	(Jn 17:23)
— He gave His Son for us	(Jn 3:16)

For us, Jesus sacrificed His life on the cross, so that our sins could be forgiven on the basis of repentance
(Lk 24:46–47)

Because of who they are, and what they have done for us, God the Father, Jesus the Son, and the Holy Spirit absolutely deserve our whole-hearted love, commitment, and service – based on the initial step of repentance

The Scriptures command us to repent:
  — Mk 1:15
  — Ac 3:19
  — Ac 17:30; 26:20

F. There is joy in heaven over every sinner who repents

(See Lk 15:5–7, 9–10, 22–4, 32)

For further consideration:

Meditate on Ro 2:4

(7)

Saving Faith

A. The second major condition to enter the Kingdom of God: saving faith

In order to be saved and to start following the Lord Jesus Christ as His disciple, the second step necessary is to believe:
Mk 1:15
Ac 20:21
Jn 3:16, 6:47
Ac 16:31
Ac 10:43, 13:38–9

B. What is saving faith?

Faith unto salvation implies various aspects, e.g.:

Believing the truth of biblical revelation	(Heb 11:1–6)
Believing the gospel	(Mk 1:15)
Believing in Jesus	(Jn 3:15)
Believing with the heart	(Ro 10:9–10)
Having faith in Jesus	(Php 3:9)
Inviting Jesus into one's heart	(Rev 3:20)
Receiving Jesus	(Jn 1:12)
Becoming obedient from one's heart	(Ro 6:17)
Putting one's trust in God	(Heb 2:13)
Having confidence in God	(1 Pe 1:21)
Setting one's hope on God	(1 Ti 4:10)

Committing one's life to God (Ps 37:5)
Faith is a gift of God (Eph 2:8; see also Jn 6:65 and Heb 12:2)

C. Examples of saving faith in the Scriptures

Nathanael	(Jn 1:45–50)
Thomas	(Jn 20:27–29)
The jailer at Philippi	(Ac 16:27–34)
One of the criminals at Calvary	(Lk 23:40–43)
Many Samaritans	(Jn 4:41–42)

Moreover: Ac 4:4, 13:12, 17:11–12, 18:8, 19:18

D. Assurance of salvation

We can be sure of our salvation (1 Jn 5:13; Ro 8:38–39; Job 19:25)
The basis for our assurance:
— trust in God and His Word (Tit 1:2, Ro 10:13)
— trust in Jesus and His Word (Rev 3:20, Jn 6:37, 10:28–29)
— the witness of the Holy Spirit in us (Ro 8:14–16, 1 Jn 3:24)
— our love for our brethren (1 Jn 3:14)
Remember:
We must never rely on our feelings, but on the facts – the reality of God and His true Word

E. A public testimony of our faith in Christ: water baptism

In the course of church history, Scriptural statements on baptism have been interpreted and expressed in a variety of practices in different denominations, movements, etc. The practice of Early Church seems to have been directed by the following guidelines:

Saving faith and water baptism go together (Mk 16:16; Ac 2:38, 41, 10:43–48, 16:14–15, 18:8)

Baptism is expected to follow salvation on the basis of repentance and saving faith (Mk 16:16, Mt 28:19)

Baptism is an outward sign of cleansing from sin (Ac 22:16), of burial with Christ (Col 2:12), and of being united with Christ into a new life (Ro 6:3–4)

F. There is great joy in salvation

Ac 8:39, 16:34
Ro 5:11
Ps 51:12

For further consideration:

Which insights on saving faith can we gain from Ro 3:21–8?

(8)

The New Birth

A. We have entered into a new life through the Holy Spirit

We have been born again (1 Pe 1:3)
We have been born of God (1 Jn 5:1)
We have the Holy Spirit living in our
  hearts (2 Co 1:22)
We have been made alive together with
  Christ (Col 2:13)
We have been raised with Christ (Eph 2:6)
We have eternal life (Jn 3:16)
We have received the witness of the Spirit (Ro 8:16)
We have been sealed with the Spirit (Eph 1:13)
We have become temples of the Spirit (1 Co 6:19)
We have been renewed by the Holy Spirit (Tit 3:5)
We have been given the mind of Christ (1 Co 2:16)
We have been consecrated (1 Co 6:11)
We have been given God's love into our
  hearts (Ro 5:5)
We have received gifts of the Spirit (1 Co 12:4–11)
We have become members of the body of
  Christ (1 Co 12:27)

B. We have entered into a new relationship with God

We know God (Jn 17:3)
We have become children of God (Jn 1:12)

We have been adopted as sons (Ro 8:15)
We have entered into the household of
  God (Eph 2:19)
We have become heirs (Ro 8:17)
We have confident access to God (Eph 3:12)
We share in the divine nature (2 Pe 1:4)
We are reconciled with God (Ro 5:10)
We have peace with God (Ro 5:1)
We are God's possession (1 Pe 2:9)

C. We have entered into a new relation to sin

We have been cleansed from sin (2 Pe 1:9)
We have been washed (1 Co 6:11)
We have died to sin (1 Pe 2:24)
We have been freed from sin (Ro 6:18)
We have a clear conscience (Heb 10:22)
We are no longer under condemnation (Ro 8:1)
We have been redeemed (Eph 1:7)
We have been forgiven (Col 1:14)
We have been saved (Eph 2:8)
We have been justified (1 Co 6:11)
We have been made righteous (1 Co 1:30)
We have laid aside our old self (Col 3:9–10)
We no longer live in the passions of the
  flesh (Eph 2:3)
We set our minds on spiritual things (Ro 8:5–6)
We have been healed (1 Pe 2:24)
We are no longer children of wrath (Eph 2:3)

D. We have entered into a new relation to the world

We have been crucified to the world   (Gal 6:14)
We have been transferred into the kingdom
    of God   (Col 1:13)
We have been seated in heavenly places   (Eph 2:6)
We have received divine citizenship   (Eph 2:19)
We have entered into the life of faith   (Gal 2:20)
We overcome the world   (1 Jn 5:4–5)
We have been given a new hope   (Col 1:27)
We are looking forward to Christ's return   (2 Pe 3:12)

For further consideration:

Why does Jesus, in Jn 3:1–21, emphasise so strongly that we need to be born again?

C.

Growing As A Disciple

(9)

Establishing a Regular Quiet Time

A. Why have a quiet time every day?

1. By meeting with God in this way, we show Him that we love Him (Consider that we were created to have fellowship with Him)
2. We cannot really get to know God if we do not have fellowship with Him often
3. These times are absolutely essential for our spiritual health and growth
   — we receive spiritual nourishment
   — we are being renewed and strengthened in our spirits
   — we get direction
   — we are being equipped to face testings and temptations

B. Two main elements of a quiet time

1. The Word of God
   Through our Bible reading, God speaks to us
2. Prayer
   Through prayer, we mainly speak to God; but we must also take time to listen to Him

C. Practical hints for planning an effective quiet time

Choose a definite place
(a quiet place, where you can meet God alone and

undisturbed; see Mt 6:6; also Mk 1:35; Mt 14:23; Lk 5:16)

Choose a definite time
— usually it is not easy to 'find' the time, therefore **make** the time
— set aside a certain period every day (see Da 6:10)
— find the time of day that is best suited for you personally
— but at the same time remember: God deserves our very best time
— the quality of our time with God is more important than the quantity
— give God enough time in order for Him to speak to you

Some suggestions for organising your devotional time
— in regard to Bible reading:
    ask the Holy Spirit to be your teacher (Ps 119:18)
    then read your Scripture passage for the day
    (see appendix, pages 120–23)
    meditate on the Word
    respond to what you have read in prayer
    write down what the Spirit particularly impressed upon you
    memorise a portion of Scripture
— in regard to prayer:
    begin with thanksgiving and praise
    confess if the Holy Spirit brings anything to your attention
    pray for your personal needs
    intercede for others
    useful: to have a list and to pray for one group of people each day, e.g. relatives, friends, home-fellowship, local church, political leaders, missionaries, etc.
    on the other hand: be open for the spontaneous guidance of the Holy Spirit

D. We must not forget:

To have a **balanced** quiet time
(there ought to be sufficient time for both Bible reading and prayer)
To look out for opportunities during the day to apply and share what we learned during our devotional time (see Jas 1:22)
To stay in prayerful contact with God during the whole day (Lk 18:1–8)
To schedule in additional times with God during the week
(for a deeper study of the Word, for more intensive prayer, etc.)

For further consideration:

Read Ex 34, especially verses 2 and 29. Are people able to recognise when you have come out of a time with God?

(10)

Getting to Know the Word of God

A. Why a disciple must get to know the Word of God

The Bible is the almighty and holy God speaking to man
Every disciple is in vital need of the Word of God
- — it is useful to teach us   (2 Ti 3:16)
- — it is useful to convict us   (2 Ti 3:16, Heb 4:12)
- — it is useful to correct us   (2 Ti 3:16)
- — it is useful to train us unto righteousness   (2 Ti 3:16)
- — it forms a basis for our faith to rest
  upon   (see Ro 10:17)
- — it edifies us   (Ac 20:32)
- — it gives peace   (Ps 119:165)
- — it communicates hope   (Ro 15:4)
- — it makes us wise   (Ps 119:98–100, 130)

B. In order to rightly understand the Word of God

We must have a teachable attitude
The Holy Spirit must be our teacher (Jn 14:26, 16:13)
We must keep three guidelines in mind:
1. Usually, the simple and obvious meaning is the intended one
   (God does not purpose to confuse us: 1 Co 14:33)
2. The context must be considered
3. The Bible itself is its best commentary

(Parallel Scripture references provide further understanding)

C. How to get to know the Word of God

1. Through hearing
2. Through reading
   — read prayerfully, asking the Holy Spirit to enlighten
     your heart and mind
   — read both the Old and New Testaments
   — follow a plan
     (see appendix, pages 120–23)
3. Through studying
   (Look at the Bereans' example in Ac 17:11)
   — Have a goal for your study
     (e.g.: Abraham as an example of faith, the life of
     Joseph, principles of prevailing prayer, how did
     Jesus teach?)

Write down discoveries that have blessed you
   — God desires to build up our knowledge of Him
   — what He reveals, we should be able to share with
     others

Methods of study
   — analysing a verse or a chapter
   — doing a character study (e.g. Simon Peter)
   — studying a certain theme (e.g. forgiveness)
4. Through meditating
   (See Jos 1:8; Ps 1:1–3)
5. Through memorising
   (Dt 6:5–6; Pr 7:1–3)
   From memorising Scripture portions, we will
   benefit in various ways:
   — Our faith will be strengthened (Mt 4:4)
   — It will help us to discern God's will (Ps 119:105)
   — The efficiency of our praying will increase

— It helps us to be victorious over sin, temptations, and
Satan
(Ps 119:11; see also Eph 6:17 and Mt 4:4, 7, 10)
Always remember:
It is important to put our knowledge of the Bible into
practice in everyday life (Jn 13:17; Jas 1:22)

For further consideration:

Why is the writer of Ps 119 so thrilled about the Word
of God?

(11)

Prayer (Part 1)

A. What is prayer?

Praying means talking with God
There are various ways of communicating with God
through prayer:

Giving Him thanks	(1 Ti 2:1)
Praising Him	(Heb 13:15)
Waiting on Him	(Ps 27:14)
Listening to Him	(Jn 10:27)
Asking Him for personal needs	(1 Sa 1:17)
Interceding for others	(1 Sa 12:19)
(see appendix, pages 124–5)	
Confessing sin	(1 Jn 1:9)
Doing spiritual warfare	(Eph 6:10–18)

B. Why should we pray?

1. Prayer is a privilege
   — in that we are allowed to come before God
   (We are sinful – God is holy; we are ignorant – God is
   omniscient)
   — in that we can evoke blessings on ourselves and
   others
2. Through prayer, we get to know God
   — the more time we spend with Him, the better we will
   know Him
   — prayer makes us understand God's plans (Ac
   10:1–20)

3. Prayer serves our spiritual well-being
    — it releases manifold blessings into our lives, e.g.
      forgiveness, comfort, strength, guidance, etc.
4. Through prayer, we can co-operate with God
    — God is committed to act in answer to prayer (Mt 7:7)
    — He is willing to change His plans in response to
      prayer (Gen 18:23–32)
      God did change His plans, for example, because of
      the prayers of Moses (Ex 32:9–14) and Hezekiah (2 Ki
      20:1–6)
    — through prayer, we can help establish God's King-
      dom (Mt 6:10)
    — through prayer, we can defeat the devil (Mt 12:29)
5. We have been commanded to pray (1 Th 5:17)
6. We should pray to see God glorified (Jn 14:13)
7. Whoever prays, brings joy to the heart of God
    (Pr 15:8)

C. The enormous possibilities of prayer

The promises:
    — anybody can pray   (Mk 11:23 : 'whoever')
    — for anything   (Mk 11:24 : 'whatever')
    — at any time   (Mk 11:25 : 'whenever')
Prayer can reach anywhere to meet any need
Prayer links us to the unlimited possibilities of God
The challenge:
    — Mt 7:7
    — Ps 2:8
    — Jer 33:3

D. Examples of great prayers in the Bible

Gen 18:16–33   (Abraham)
Ex 32:7–14   (Moses)

2 Sa 7:18–29   (David)
1 Ki 8:12–53   (Solomon)
Ezr 9:5–15   (Ezra)
Ne 1:4–11   (Nehemiah)
Da 9:3–19   (Daniel)
Jn 17:1–26   (the Lord Jesus)

For further consideration:

What can we learn about the nature and possibilities of prayer from Jesus' words in Mk 11:22–26?

(12)

Prayer (Part 2)

A. Hindrances to prayer

Unconfessed sin	(Isa 59:1–2)
Unforgiveness	(Mk 11:25)
A wrong motivation	(Jas 4:3)
Doubt	(Jas 1:6–8)
Unbelief	(Heb 11:6)
Slackness	(Jas 4:2)

B. The devil seeks to keep us from praying

Satan fears praying people, because
— prayer brings power into our life and work for God
— prayer is the most powerful tool to defeat the enemy's purposes
— he has already been much harmed through praying people

Therefore, Satan tries hard to eliminate our power in prayer

(for instance through distractions, temptations, evil thoughts, condemnation, sowing of doubt, despair)

We need to watch and pray (Mt 26:41)

And we must resist the devil (1 Pet 5:8–9; Jas 4:7)

C. Two cornerstones for confidence in prayer

1. God's character:
   — His commitment: He has promised to answer
     prayer   (Jer 33:3)
   — His omnipotence: He **can** answer prayer   (Ge 18:14)
   — His love: He **desires to** answer prayer   (Jer 29:11–14)
   — His faithfulness: He **is going to** answer
     prayer   (1 Ki 8:56)
2. Our sonship
   — we have been adopted as sons   (Ro 8:15)
   — we have access to the Father   (Eph 3:12)
   — our father wishes to bless us   (Mt 7:7–11)
   — our Father wants to give us a prayer
     inheritance   (Ps 2:8)

D. The all-important help of the Holy Spirit

We need Him to give us a 'spirit of
  prayer'   (Zec 12:10)
We need His power to strengthen us   (Ro 8:26)
We need His wisdom to direct us   (Ro 8:26–27)
We need to pray 'in the Spirit'   (Eph 6:18)

E. Principles of prevailing prayer

Because prayer is so powerful, the Bible instructs us
thoroughly how we can pray effectively:
With a clear conscience   (1 Jn 3:21–22)
According to God's will   (Mt 6:10)
Abiding in Jesus   (Jn 15:7)
In the name of Jesus   (Jn 14:13)
In the Spirit   (Eph 6:18)

In faith   (Mt 21:22)
Appealing to God's character   (Ge 18:25)
Pleading God's promises   (Ex 32:13)
Moreover, see Jas 4:3; Pr 21:13; 1 Pe 3:7; Heb 4:16; Ps
100:4

F. Like the Lord Jesus, we need to be determined to pray

To Him, prayer was of the utmost importance
— His life and ministry were 'bathed' in prayer (Lk 3:21;
6:12; 9:16; 9:29; 22:17–19; 22:41–46; 23:34; 24:50–51)
— He regarded prayer as more important than food (Mt
4:2), sleep (Lk 6:12), and public ministry (Lk 5:15–16)
He **made** time to pray (Mk 1:35; Mt 14:23; Lk 5:16)
He is interceding for the believers right now (Heb
7:25, Ro 8:34)

For further consideration:

In what respects is the Lord's Prayer (Mt 6:9–13) **the**
model prayer?

(13)

The Person and Ministry of the Holy Spirit

A. The Holy Spirit as a member of the Trinity

The Holy Spirit is not just an influence, but a person
— He is the third member of the threefold Godhead
Like God the Father and God the Son, the Holy Spirit
is eternal (Heb 9:14), omnipresent (Ps 139:7), omniscient (1 Co 2:10), and omnipotent (Lk 1:35)
He shows personality attributes
— intellect   (Ro 8:27)
— sensitivity   (Eph 4:30)
— will   (1 Co 12:11)

B. The Bible mentions the Holy Spirit in various ways

Through different names, e.g.:
— the Spirit of God   (Mt 3:16)
— the Spirit of Christ   (Ro 8:9)
— the good Spirit   (Neh 9:20)
— comforter, counsellor   (Jn 14:16, 26)
— the Spirit of truth   (Jn 14:17)
— the Spirit of adoption   (Ro 8:15)
— the Spirit of grace   (Heb 10:29)
Through symbols:
— dove   (Mt 3:16)
— wind   (Ac 2:2)
— voice   (1 Ki 19:12)

— oil	(1 Sa 16:13)
— water	(Isa 44:3; Jn 7:37–39)
— seal	(Eph 1:13)
— fire	(Ac 2:3)

C. The work of the Holy Spirit in the believer

He convicts	(Jn 16:8–11)
He brings about the new birth	(Jn 3:5–8)
He gives us assurance of salvation	(Ro 8:16)
He lives in us	(Jn 14:17)
He teaches us	(Jn 14:26; 16:13–14)
He helps us	(Ro 8:26)
He sanctifies us	(Ro 15:16)
He brings about the fruit of the Spirit	(Gal 5:22–23)
He bestows various gifts	(1 Co 12:4–11)
He speaks through us	(Mk 13:11)
He gives us power to witness	(Ac 1:8)

Moreover, see Jn 14:16; Ro 5:5; 1 Th 1:6; Ro 14:17; Ro 15:13; Mt 12:28

D. All believers are to be filled with the Holy Spirit (Eph 5:18)

Some examples of Spirit-filled lives in the Bible:

— David	(1 Sa 16:13)
— the Lord Jesus	(Lk 4:1, 14)
— the apostles	(Ac 2:2–4)
— Paul	(Ac 9:17)

There are hindrances to leading a life in the fullness of the Spirit, e.g. disobedience (Ac 5:32), pride (1 Pe 5:5), lack of faith (Heb 11:6), an evil motivation (Ac 8:18–24)

Steps for entering into the Spirit-filled life
  — cleansing from sin through repentance and con-
    fession (1 Jn 1:9)
  — asking to be filled (1 Jn 5:14–15) according to God's
    command in Eph 5:18
  — believing (Heb 11:6; Mk 11:24)
    (note the Lord Jesus' special promise in Lk 11:13)
The original text of Eph 5:18 makes it clear that for a
Christian to be filled with the Spirit is not to be a
one-time experience; rather, he is to go on being
filled continuously
  (notice the example of Simon Peter, who was filled in Ac
  2:4 and again in Ac 4:31)

For further consideration:

Study Paul's teaching about the Holy Spirit in Ro
8:1–17, 26–27

(14)

Praise

A. What is praise?

Focusing on God for who He is (1 Ch 29:10–13)
Acknowledging God for His wonderful character
and deeds (Isa 25:1)
Making known the excellence of God (1 Pe 2:9)
Giving glory to Him (Ps 29:1)
Honouring Him (Da 4:34)
Magnifying Him (Ps 34:3)
Exalting Him (Ps 99:5)
Expressing admiration of Him (2 Th 1:10)

B. Why should we praise?

Man was created to praise God (Eph 1:3–14)
Nothing else can praise God like
man (Ps 30:9; 115:17–18)
God is all worthy to receive our praise (Rev 5:9–14)
Praise is a sacrifice which pleases
God (Heb 13:15–16)
In order to declare God's greatness before the
world (Ps 66:5–8)
To celebrate His mighty acts in the past (Ps 98:1)
God dwells in the praise of His people (Ps 22:3)
Praise releases blessings on us (Ps 67:5–6)
It builds our faith (Ro 4:20)
We have been commanded to praise (Ps 146:1; 100:4)

C. When should we praise?

At all times   (Ps 34:1; 145:2)
In all circumstances   (Heb 13:15)
  (consider the example of Paul and Silas: Ac 16:25)

D. How can we praise?

With words   (Ps 9:1)
In song   (Ps 104:33)
With instruments   (Ps 150:3–5)
Bowing down   (Ps 95:6)
With hands raised   (Ps 134:2)
Dancing   (Ps 150:4)

E. Some suggestions what to praise for

God the Father: His greatness, majesty, holiness, love, faithfulness, justice, mercy, wisdom, omnipotence, miracles, promises
God the Son: His sacrifice, redemption, victory, blood, name, example, humility, meekness, compassion, lordship over all
God the Spirit: His presence, gentleness, comfort, teaching, regenerating and sanctifying power, fruit, gifts

F. It is important to have the right attitude

With a sincere heart   (Ps 119:7)
With all one's heart   (Ps 138:1)

In spirit   (Jn 4:23–24)
In truth   (Jn 4:23–24)

G. Great Scriptures of praise

Ex 15:1–18
1 Sa 2:1–10
Ne 9:6–37
Ps 103; 147; 148; 150
Lk 1:46–55
Ro 11:33–36
Rev 7:9–12

For further consideration:

Meditate on the great song of praise in 1 Ch 16:8–36

(15)

Involvement in a Local Church

A. Why should we be involved in a local church?

Where we gather with other Christians in Jesus' name, we will meet Jesus Himself (Mt 18:20)
For our spiritual growth, we need the grace of God as it manifests itself in the lives of our brethren (consider Heb 10:25)
— we can enjoy fellowship with brothers and sisters in Christ
— we receive instruction, direction, correction, etc.
— our faith gets strengthened
— prayer support is available
— we can receive counsel and help
The church offers us opportunities to use our spiritual gifts
— we can bless others through gifts/ministries God has given us
— if we do not pass on what we have received, we will spiritually decline

B. Some traits of a dynamic biblical church

A total commitment to the lordship of Christ
Love and unity amongst the members
A strong emphasis on prayer
Worship
Moving in the power of the Holy Spirit, and
  exercising His gifts

Encouraging holy living
Calling sinners to repentance
Preaching the gospel of salvation
Abounding in good works, also towards the needy
Sacrificial giving
Intense involvement in missions
Looking for and hastening Christ's return

C. Principles of true fellowship amongst Christians

Loving one another	(Jn 13:34)
Preferring one another	(Ro 12:10)
Encouraging one another	(Heb 3:13)
Edifying one another	(Ro 14:19)
Comforting one another	(1 Th 4:18)
Forgiving one another	(Eph 4:32)
Serving one another	(Gal 5:13)
Carrying one another's burdens	(Gal 6:2)
Teaching one another	(Col 3:16)
Exhorting one another	(Col 3:16)
Praying for one another	(Jas 5:16)
Offering one another hospitality	(1 Pe 4:9)

See also: Ro 15:7; 1 Pe 5:5; Eph 5:21; Eph 4:2; Heb 10:24; Ac 2:42–47

D. Areas of possible involvement in a local church

Seek God, and then talk with your pastor/leader to find out what kind of involvement God intends for you

Some possibilities are: praying intensely for your church, practical help, children's work, Bible class, youth group, home fellowship, teaching the Word, music, evangelistic team, literature distribution

E. How should we be involved?

Out of love	(1 Co 13:1–3)
As unto the Lord	(1 Co 10:31)
Prayerfully	(1 Th 5:17)
In humility	(Mt 11:29)
Joyfully	(Php 4:4)

For further consideration:

Which guidelines for local church life can we find in Ro 12:9–21; 1 Th 5:14–24; and 1 Co 13:4–7?

(16)

Growing in Faith

A. We find various kinds of faith in the Bible

Saving faith   (Jn 3:16)
The gift of faith   (1 Co 12:9)
Active faith   (Jn 14:12; Mk 11:23)
(In the following, the focus will be on this third type of faith)

B. What is active faith?

It is not a matter of the mind, but an act of the will (Pr 3:5)
It means unwavering trust, absolute confidence
It is based on God's character (Ps 9:10) and on His Word (see Ro 10:17)
It is always active in the present
(It believes that God keeps His promises **now**, that He answers prayer **now**, that He intervenes **now**, etc.)

C. Examples of active faith in the Scriptures

Abraham   (Ro 4:19–21)
Joshua   (Jos 10:12–14)
David   (1 Sa 17:45–47)
Daniel   (Da 6:23)
the Lord Jesus   (Jn 11:40–44)

Simon Peter   (Ac 9:32–34)
Paul   (Ac 27:25)

D. Some hindrances to active faith

A guilty conscience   (1 Jn 3:21)
Fear   (Jn 14:1; Mk 4:40)
Doubt   (Jas 1:6–8; Mk 11:23)
Seeking glory from men   (Jn 5:44)
Presumption   (Pr 3:5; Jos 7:2–5)

E. How can my faith grow?

1. Through feeding much on the Word of God
   — getting to know God's character (meditating, for
     example, on Ps 146)
   — gathering a treasure of biblical promises and prin-
     ciples in my heart
2. By studying God's ways with man
   — in the Bible (e.g. Heb 12:5–11)
   — considering God's dealings in the lives of other
     Christians, past and present
   — reflecting on the way God has led me so far
3. Through giving myself to prayer
   — look at the examples of Jehoshaphat (2 Ch 20:1–3),
     Hezekiah (2 Ki 19:14–20), and David (1 Sa 30:4, 6)
4. By giving glory to God (Ro 4:20)
5. Through welcoming God-given faith challenges
   (Consider David's example in 1 Sa 17:32, 37,
   45–46)
6. By learning the secret of growing in faith:
   Faith does not grow on the basis of self-effort, but
   through my looking unto Jesus/God

— Jesus is the author and perfecter of our faith (Heb 12:2)
— We are to 'take hold on the faithfulness of God' (alternative translation for Mk 11:22)

F. Strong active faith accomplishes great things

Isa 30:15
Jn 14:12
Mk 9:23
1 Jn 5:4

For further consideration:

By a careful study of Ps 78, what active faith principles can be discovered?

(17)

Principles of Guidance

A. It is essential to discover God's will for our lives

God has a plan for each person's life (Ps 139:16; Jer 1:5)

As a loving Father, God desires our total well-being on the basis of our living in accordance with His will for us (Dt 28:1–2, 15)

He does not hide His will from us; rather, He wants to reveal Himself and His intentions for us (Heb 11:6; Jas 1:5)

He wants us to be intelligent in our decision-making (Ps 32:8–9)

Our obedience or disobedience to the will of God often affects not only our life, but also the lives of others (Jos 6:18; 7:1–26)

B. It is possible to find out God's will for us

The directions for most areas of our lives have already been clearly defined in the Word of God (Consider e.g. the Ten Commandments [Ex 20:1–17] and the Sermon on the Mount [Mt 5–7])

But there are other areas, where we need to particularly seek God's guidance as to what specific direction He wants us to take (e.g.: what job to choose, whom to marry)

God offers to guide us in specifics (Ps 25:12; 32:8)

C. We must come prepared in order to be able to discern God's will

A genuine willingness to do His will (Ro 12:1–2, see also Mt 6:33)
Obedience (Ps 25:10)
Humility (Ps 25:9)
Listening to God in prayer (Pr 8:34)
Trusting Him (Pr 3:5–7)

D. There are three main ways to receive divine guidance

1. Through the Word of God (Ps 119:9–11, 105)
2. Through the speaking of the Holy Spirit (see Ac 11:12; 13:2; 16:6–7)
3. Through the counsel of men and women of God (see Pr 12:15)

E. A practical checklist for determining guidance

Have I been obedient to the guidance which God has already given me?
Am I willing to give up my personal desires, and to absolutely do God's will?
What does the Word of God say in regard to my present situation?
Have I approached the question on hand with earnest, persistent, and believing prayer?
Have I received confirmation from my spiritual leaders?

Am I about to act out of a momentary feeling or impression?

Do I tend to limit God's guidance through my intellect?

Do I too much expect God to lead me in extraordinary ways?

Can I recognise confirmation or obstacles in the circumstances?

What does my God-given common sense say?

Have I chosen the timing according to God's schedule?

How has God led other Christians in similar situations?

Does that which I believe to have discerned as guidance from God violate any principle of His Word?

F. Always remember:

God intends at all times the very best for us

God never makes any mistakes

God is never in a hurry

God's peace in the heart will confirm the right decision (Isa 26:3, Php 4:7)

True fulfilment and happiness is only in doing God's will

Doing God's will means to do the right thing, in the right place, at the right time, with the right attitude of heart

For further consideration:

In what respects can Eliezer's guidance in Gen 24:1–61 be regarded as exemplary for us?

(18)

Testings and Temptations

A. God tests us for good purposes

He tests us because He seeks to bless us
— He wants to prepare us so that we can receive more of the good which He has in store for us
— He seeks to expose weaknesses in us so that we discover where we need more of His grace (2 Ch 32:31, Dt 8:2)

In testing us, God may particularly intend
— to teach us	(Dt 8:3)
— to strengthen our trust in Him	(1 Pe 1:6–7)
— to build our character	(Jas 1:2–4)
— to purify us	(Ps 66:10)
— to increase our diligence in prayer	(Lk 11:5–9; Mt 15:21–28)
— to humble us	(Dt 8:2)
— to discipline us	(Dt 8:5)

Men of the Bible who passed God's testing in specific areas
— Abraham: obedience	(Gen 22:1–19)
— Joseph: faith	(Gen 37:5–9, 28; 39:20; 41:40)
— David: patience	(1 Sa 16:12–13; 2 Sa 5:4)
— Caleb: endurance	(Jos 14:6–14)

A key to stand firm in God's testings:
With the help of the grace of God, we need to cultivate the attributes mentioned in 2 Pe 1:5–9: diligence, faith, virtue, knowledge, self-control, patience, godliness, brotherly kindness, love

B. Satan tempts us for evil purposes

He tempts us because he seeks to destroy us
  — he wants us to miss the mark of God's loving inten-
    tions of us
  — he wants us to be burdened with guilt
  — he wants to see our confidence in God broken down
  — he wants us to serve him
  — he wants to lead us into bondage
  — he wants us to perish

Satan tempts us through various avenues, e.g.:
  — not loving God first and foremost   (Mt 4:9)
  — pride   (Ac 12:21–23)
  — physical desires   (Mt 4:3)
  — fleshly passions   (1 Cor 7:5)
  — sexual immorality   (Gen 39:7–10)
  — disobedience   (Gen 3:1–7)
  — murmuring   (1 Co 10:10)
  — love of money   (Jn 12:6)

Two keys to overcome the devil's temptations:
1. Our determination
  — being watchful and prayerful   (Mk 14:38)
  — not giving Satan an opportunity   (Eph 4:27)
  — putting on the whole spiritual armour   (Eph 6:11)
  — resisting the devil   (Jas 4:7)
2. The helping presence of Jesus
  — He was tempted in all respects as we are   (Heb 4:15)
  — therefore, He is able to help us in our
    temptations   (Heb 2:18)
  — we are to look up to Jesus in faith   (Heb 12:2)

C. If we do fail in testing or temptation, we can be restored

The necessary steps are: confession, repentance, being cleansed, being forgiven (1 Jn 1:9)

D. Very important:

Whether we face testing or temptation, God is always in control
- — He never allows us to be tempted beyond our capacity (1 Co 10:13)
- — He also provides a way out (1 Co 10:13)

Temptation in itself is not sin; if, however, we yield to it, it becomes sin

For further consideration:

What does Jas 1:12–16 state about God testing us only for our good, but the devil tempting us for evil?

(19)

Stewardship

A. We have been appointed to be stewards

Everything we have, we received from God (Ac 17:25)

God is the owner, we are His stewards (see Mt 25:14)

Stewardship implies both privilege and responsibility

God will hold us accountable for how we handle what He has entrusted to us (Ro 14:12)

B. Jesus emphasised the necessity of good stewardship

Lk 19:11–27

Lk 12:42–48

Lk 16:1, 2

Lk 16:10–12

C. What is expected of a good steward?

He must be dedicated to his master (Mt 25:24–27, 30)

He must manage the master's household

He must act in the owner's interest (Mt 25:20–21, 27)

He must be faithful (Lk 16:10–12)

D. Essential areas for stewardship

1. The responsible use of time
   — time is valuable
     (Our life is short; wasted time can never be bought back)
   — time has been entrusted to us for a purpose (1 Co 10:31)
   — misuse or waste of time plays into the devil's hands
   — instead, we are to make the most of our time (Eph 5:15–16)
   — we should act not on the basis of pressure, but on the basis of priorities (first: our relationship to God; second: our family; third: our spiritual ministry; fourth: our job; fifth: other activities)
   — we always have enough time to do what is God's will for us
   — to pray means to save time
2. The responsible use of money
   — we are to lay up treasures not on earth, but in heaven (Mt 6:19–20)
     (dangers of wealth: Mt 6: 21, 24; Mk 4:19, 1 Ti 6:9)
   — as Christians, we should tithe as well as give offerings to God (there is a danger of robbing God: Mal 3:8–10)
   — tithing, that is giving a tenth to God, is not a donation to God, but merely the due recognition of His ownership (see Pr 3:9)
   — we are to give to God: willingly (1 Ch 29:3, 5, 9), regularly (1 Co 16:2), sacrificially (Lk 21:1–4), joyfully (2 Co 9:7)
   — giving is more blessed than receiving (Ac 20:35)
3. Presenting our body to God (Ro 12:1)
   — we are the temple of the Holy Spirit (1 Co 3:16)
   — we are to yield the members of our body not to sin, but to God (Ro 6:13)
   — we should live in a healthy way (Mk 6:31; Lk 21:34)
4. Serving others with our spiritual gifts (1 Pe 4:10)

— the various gifts of the Spirit (1 Co 12:1–11) are meant to edify and equip the body of Christ (Ro 12:4–8; 1 Co 14:12)
5. Using our home for God
— an open door for those seeking help or counsel
— a place where hospitality is offered
— a venue for home fellowship meetings

E. Rewards for good stewardship

Lk 16:10–12
Mt 25:20–23
Mt 25:31–40

For further consideration:

Meditate on 1 Co 4:1–2

(20)

Holiness and Sanctification

A. The holiness of God

God is holy (1 Pe 1:16; Lev 20:26)
From the Scriptures it seems that God's holiness is
the characteristic of His personality (see Ex 3:5; Isa
6:3; Rev 4:8; the Bible mentions God's holiness far
more often than His love, for instance)
God's holiness means 'otherness', His being 'separated from' all that is imperfect or unclean; He is
perfect, pure, blameless, excellent, and worthy to be
met with reverence and awe

B. God desires us to be holy

1 Pe 1:15; Eph 1:4; Lev 11:44–45

C. Why should we lead holy lives?

As Christians, through our new birth, we have been
set apart to live in such a way that people will
recognise we are living 'separated from' the world
and 'reserved for' God
  — if we are true children of our holy Father God, we
    should show the family characteristic of holiness
    (Heb 12:10; 1 Pe 2:9)
  — Jesus sacrificed Himself, that we would live in holi-
    ness (Col 1:22)

— He who abides in Him, should live as He lived (1 Jn 2:6)
— a holy life-style releases blessings into our lives (see Dt 26:16–19)
— it is the best qualification to be a blessing to others (1 Pe 3:1)
— holy living on earth prepares us for heaven (Heb 12:14; Rev 21:27)

D. What does sanctification mean?

Generally speaking, sanctification can be understood as
— the process of becoming holy in our whole Christian walk (1 Pe 1:15)
— progressively coming to be more godly in character (Eph 5:1)
— growing up into the likeness of Christ (Eph 4:15)
— the ongoing change into Christ's glorious perfection (2 Co 3:18)

E. God desires our sanctification

1 Th 4:3; 2 Th 2:13; Jn 17:17, 19

F. There are three divine agents in our sanctification

God the Father	(1Th 5:23)
The Holy Spirit	(2 Th 2:13; Ro 15:16)
The Lord Jesus	(1 Co 1:30; Eph 5:26)

G. Means for our sanctification

Our sanctification takes place
in Christ	(1 Co 1:2)
through Jesus' sacrifice	(Heb 10:10)
by His blood	(Heb 13:12)
in the truth	(Jn 17:17)
by the Word of God	(1 Ti 4:5)
by faith	(Ac 26:18)

H. It is our responsibility to be committed to a holy and sanctified life (2 Cor 7:1)

Let us walk
in Christ	(Col 2:6)
in the Spirit	(Gal 5:16)
in humility	(Mic 6:8)
in honesty	(Ro 13:13)
in obedience	(2 Jn 6)
in love	(Eph 5:2)
in the truth	(3 Jn 4)
in the light	(1 Jn 1:7)

For further consideration:

Which insights into holiness and sanctification can we gain from studying 1 Pe 1 to 3?

D.
Serving As A Disciple

(21)

Loving God

A. What is love?

It is not primarily a feeling, but an action of the will
It is the determination to seek the other's best
To love God means to live to please Him through putting Him and His desires first in our lives
The Holy Spirit equips us with such unselfish love (Ro 5:5; Gal 5:22)

B. God deserves our love

He is the most loveable being (1 Jn 4:8)
He first loved us (1 Jn 4:10)
He loved us so much that He gave His only Son for us (Jn 3:16)
He surrounds us with His perfect love every day (Ps 23:6)

C. How can we express our love for God?

1. Through our gratitude for who He is
   (Think of His love, goodness, mercy, compassion, faithfulness, justice, willingness to forgive, etc.)
2. Through our rejoicing over Him
   — because of His wonderful character
   — because of His great deeds

3. Through our desire to commune with Him
    — in that we wish to get to know Him better (especially from His Word)
    — in that we offer Him our fellowship in prayer
4. Through living in such a way that we bring joy to Him
    — by making important for ourselves what is important to Him
      (e.g. growing into Christlikeness, showing justice and mercy, helping fulfil the Great Commission)
    — by making Him happy through our life-style
      (pursuing a holy way of life in thought and deed)
    — by helping ease His burden over this world
        see Lk 13:34; Ac 9:4
        we can change the world through prayer (Mt 6:9–10)
    — by our willingness to make sacrifices for God
        see the example of the widow in Mk 12:41–44
        God gave His most precious – His Son – for us
        What are we willing to give to Him?
5. Through our obedience to His Word
        Jn 14:15; Mt 7:21–23
6. Through telling Him that we love Him
    — in prayer and praise
    — through word and song

D. All our work for God must be based on love for Him

What is not done out of love, profits nothing (1 Co 13:1–3)

True love for God is **the** test of our commitment to Him

(Consider how deeply Jesus tested Simon Peter's love for Him in Jn 21:15–17)

To truly love God with all our being, is the greatest
commandment of all (Mt 22:35–38; Dt 6:4–7)

E. Blessings that follow those who love God

God loves them   (Pr 8:17)
God keeps covenant and mercy with them   (Dt 7:9)
God protects them   (Ps 145:20)
God works in everything for their good   (Ro 8:28)
God has wonderful things prepared for
  them   (1 Co 2:9)
God blesses them for a thousand generations
                                             (Ex 20:6)

For further consideration:

God appreciates signs of our love for Him; study the
example in Mk 14:3–9

(22)

Having a Servant's Heart

A. To become great in God's Kingdom, we must become servants

Mk 9:33–35
Mk 10:35–45
Lk 22:27
Jn 13:12–17

B. Marks of a true servant

He is unselfish
He is determined to give rather than receive
He is sensitive towards the needs of others (Php 2:4)
He is willing to carry the burdens of others (Gal 6:2)
He is indifferent towards public recognition (Mt 6:33)
He gives God all the glory (1 Co 4:7; 2 Co 10:17)
He is humble (Eph 4:2)
In all: He humbly gives himself in service to the needs of others

C. True servants in the Bible

Joshua	(Nu 11:28)
Elisha	(1 Ki 19:21)
Andrew	(Jn 1:41–42; 12:20–22)
Tabitha	(Ac 9:36–39)

D. Jesus as the greatest example of true servanthood

He humbled Himself to become a servant to
   men   (Php 2:7)
  — He provided wine   (Jn 2:1–8)
  — He broke the bread   (Mt 14:19, Lk 24:30)
  — He prepared breakfast   (Jn 21:5, 9–13)
  — He healed the sick   (Mk 3:10; Mt 8:14–16)
  — He comforted a mother   (Lk 7:12–15)
  — He blessed little children   (Mt 19:13–15)
He even humbled Himself to render a slave's service
to His disciples (Jn 13:1–17)

E. A servant cannot serve two masters (Lk 16:13)

Do we serve God's Kingdom or ourselves? (Mt 6:33;
Mk 10:37)
Do we serve God or mammon? (Mt 6:24)
We are expected to serve God, and Him only (1 Co
4:1)
(Consider Joshua's example in Jos 24:15)

F. God resists the proud, but gives His grace to the humble (1 Pe 5:5)

God hates pride (Pr 8:13), and desires humility (Mic
6:8)
He resisted the pride of Uzziah (2 Ch 26:16),
Nebuchadnezzar (Da 4:24–33), and Herod (Ac 12:21–
23)
But He blessed and raised up the humble, e.g. Moses
(Nu 12:3), Daniel (Da 2:30), and Paul (Ac 20:19)

Spiritual leadership is impossible without humility:
Lk 14:11

G. Rewards of a servant of God

He is not expected to be 'successful' as much as to be
faithful (1 Co 4:2)
He who truly serves, serves the Lord Jesus (Mt
25:31–40)
His satisfaction is in pleasing his Lord (2 Ti 2:4)
His Master will reward him (Mt 25:21)

H. We need to learn to be humble

Jesus said we must learn humility from Him (Mt
11:29)
Therefore, we should
— humble ourselves before God (1 Pe 5:6)
— ask God to give us grace that a humble disposition of
   heart will be established into our character

For further consideration:

According to Php 2:5–11, which attitude are we
challenged to have?

(23)

Gifts of the Spirit

A. The Holy Spirit equips believers to accomplish their God-given tasks

He bestows:

the fruit of the Spirit	(Gal 5:22–23)
diverse ministries	(1 Co 12:28; Eph 4:11)
diverse operations	(Ro 12:6–8)
various gifts of grace	(1 Co 12:8–10)

(In the following, these gifts will be further considered)

B. Gifts of revelation

1. The word of knowledge (1 Co 12:8)
   Definition: through divine revelation, knowing certain facts regarding a person or situation
   Examples: Joseph (Ge 41:25–32), Elisha (2 Ki 6:8–12), Jesus (Jn 4:17–18), Jesus (Mt 21:2–3)
2. The word of wisdom (1 Co 12:8)
   Definition: through divine revelation, declaring thoughts and plans of God as a help to handle a particular situation
   Examples: Solomon (1 Ki 3:24–28), Jesus (Jn 8:4–7), Jesus (Lk 20:20–26), Gamaliel (Ac 5:38–39)
3. The discerning of spirits (1 Co 12:10)
   Definition: through divine revelation, having insight into what spirit is actuating a certain person or situation
   Examples: Jesus (Mt 12:34), Jesus (Lk 13:11–16), Jesus (Jn 8:44), Paul (Ac 13:6–12)

C. Gifts of power

1. Faith (1 Co 12:9)
   Definition: a divine enabling to trust and be assured that God is going to prove His power in a certain situation
   Examples: Joshua (Jos 10:12–14), Elijah (1 Ki 18:17–40), Jesus (Mk 4:37–40), Jesus (Jn 11:41–44)
2. Healing (1 Co 12:9)
   Definition: a divine enabling to impart God's power to heal
   Examples: Jesus (Mk 1:29–31), Jesus (Mk 3:1–5), Philip (Ac 8:6–7), Paul (Ac 14:9–10)
3. Working of miracles (1 Co 12:10)
   Definition: a divine enabling to perform supernatural acts
   Examples: Elisha (2 Ki 4:1–7), Jesus (Jn 2:1–11), Jesus (Lk 9:16–17), Stephen (Ac 6:8)

D. Gifts of utterance

1. Prophecy (1 Co 12:10)
   Definition: communicating a revealed message from the heart of God into a certain situation (sometimes relating to future events)
   Examples: Isaiah (Mt 13:14), Jesus (Mt 24:3–42), Jesus (Jn 21:18), Agabus (Ac 11:27–28)
   Scripture guideline: 1 Co 14:1–6, 22–33, 39–40
2. Tongues (1 Co 12:10)
   Definition: being able to express oneself in an unknown heavenly tongue
   Examples: the apostles (Ac 2:4) – believers in Cornelius' home (Ac 10:46) – disciples in Ephesus (Ac 19:6) – Paul (1 Co 14:18)
   Scripture guideline: 1 Co 14:1–28

3. Interpretation of tongues (1 Co 12:10)
   Definition: being able to share the meaning of unknown
   tongues in an understandable language
   Scripture guideline: 1 Co 14:13, 26–28

For further consideration:

Which gifts became manifest in Simon Peter's ministry as recorded in Ac 2–5 and 10?

(24)

Spiritual Warfare

A. Know the enemy

Our fight is against the evil forces of darkness (Eph 6:12)
Our main adversary is Satan
In the Scriptures, he is mentioned as:
— devil   (1 Pe 5:8)
— accuser   (Rev 12:10)
— tempter   (Mt 4:3)
— liar   (Jn 8:44)
— murderer   (Jn 8:44)
— serpent   (Ge 3:1)
— angel of light   (2 Co 11:14)
— the evil one   (1 Jn 2:14)

B. Know how the enemy attacks

The devil is constantly out to destroy the Christian (1 Pe 5:8)
He is cunning in his tactics (Eph 6:11; Ge 3:1–6)
He chooses circumstances that seem favourable for his evil plans (Mt 4:2–3)
Some of his ways of attack:
— the main battle-field is our mind:
— he accuses   (Zec 3:1)
— he deceives   (2 Co 11:14)
— he tempts   (1 Th 3:5)
— he inspires evil thoughts, confusion, doubt, fear, despair etc.   (Mt 16:23; Ac 5:3)

93

— he appeals to fleshly desires   (Gal 5:17)
— he also seeks entry into the lives of people through their involvement with cults, drugs, idolatry, ancestral worship, witchcraft or other occult practices (Ac 16:16–18; 1 Sa 28:6–19, 15:22, 23)
— he troubles people through demons (see Lk 13:10–16)

We must not be ignorant of Satan's evil schemes (see 2 Co 2:11)

C. Know your weapons

Our armour is not carnal, but spiritual (2 Co 10:4)
According to Eph 6:14–18, it consists of:
— the girdle of truth
— the breastplate of righteousness
— the shoes of the gospel of peace
— the shield of faith
— the helmet of salvation
— the sword of the Word of God
— prayer

As soldiers of Christ, we must be on the alert
— we must be sober and watchful (1 Pe 5:8)
— we must not give Satan any opportunity (Eph 4:27)
— we must put on the **whole** armour (Eph 6:13)
— we must actively resist the devil (Jas 4:7)
— we must take the offensive and use the sword of the Word (Mt 4:4, 7, 10)
— we must fight against Satan the fight of faith (1 Pe 5:9)

D. Know that Satan is a defeated foe

The decisive and final victory over Satan was won on the cross (Col 2:14–15)
Satan has been defeated once and for all (Heb 2:14–15)

All his fights now, as he still rules this world (Jn 14:30), are fights of retreat
His final destiny has already been decided (Mt 25:41; Rev 12:9–10)

E. Know that you have been given authority over Satan

Jesus has given us all the authority necessary (Lk 10:19)
The Holy Spirit in us is stronger than Satan in the world (1 Jn 4:4)
There is overcoming power in the blood of Jesus (Rev 12:11), the name of Jesus (Php 2:9–10), our testimony (Rev 12:11), and our faith (1 Jn 5:4)
When we resist the devil, he will flee (Jas 4:7)
We can bind Satan (Mt 18:18)
We can destroy strongholds of the enemy (2 Co 10:4)
Remember: victory for us is only possible through Christ
(1 Co 15:57)

For further consideration:

What does Mt 4:1–11 teach us about spiritual warfare?

(25)

Spiritual Leadership in the Family

A. The importance of the family unit

The family was instituted by God (Ge 1:27–28)
The family is God's design for the multiplication of mankind (Ge 1:28)
The family is meant to be the natural training ground for our children
The family is the most natural environment for spiritual growth
The family is the smallest cell of 'Kingdom living'
A godly family life is a strong protection in today's world (Ps 91)

B. The biblical order of the family

Christ is the head of the husband (1 Co 11:3)
The husband is the head of the wife (1 Co 11:3; Eph 5:21–25)
— the husband is expected to love his wife (Eph 5:25)
— the wife is expected to submit to her husband (1 Pe 3:1)

C. The parents carry spiritual responsibility for their children

Parents do not own their children; God has entrusted the parents as stewards

The parents are to help develop the children's God-given potential

They are to raise their children in a godly way (Eph 6:4)

The parental influence is of the utmost importance with regard to the eternal destiny of the children (Pr 22:6)

The aim of all child-raising should be to present the children mature in Christ for service to God

D. How a father can practice spiritual leadership in the home

1. Through living as a godly example (1 Pe 5:3)
   (The father should, for instance, show God's love, goodness, kindness, justice, and willingness to forgive)
2. Through functioning as a 'priest' for his family (1 Pe 2:9)
   — he represents God before them
     (especially through teaching them the Word of God; see Dt 5:5)
   — he represents them before God
     (praying for them)
3. Through giving spiritual direction
   (e.g. counsel on tithing, which church to attend, etc.)
4. Through making the salvation of his children a primary concern
5. Through the use of parental authority/discipline
   — God disciplines us because He loves us (Heb 12:6)
   — absence of parental discipline spoils the child (Pr 29:21)
     (If the parents refrain from taking directive influence over the child's life – the devil certainly won't!)

— the child must experience that we discipline misbe-
haviour, but that we still love him nevertheless

E. Blessings that follow godly leadership in the home

The parents will have a clear conscience before God
(Pr 23:24)
Iniquity will be averted from the children (Ex 20:5–6)
The children can live blessed lives (Pr 20:7)
The children are being led on the way to God (Pr 22:6)
The parents leave their children a godly example
(2 Ti 1:5)
They leave them a good reputation (Pr 17:6)
They bring about manifold blessings through their
prayers (2 Sa 7:25, 1 Ki 8:20)

For further consideration:

Study the examples of Abraham (Ge 18:19), David (1
Ki 2:1–4; 3:3), and Lois/Eunice (2 Ti 1:5; 3:15)

(26)

Co-operating in a Home Fellowship

A. The home group as a means towards spiritual growth

We cannot reach spiritual maturity on our own; we need the fellowship of others to help us grow into Christlikeness (Eph 4:11–16)

Whatever the name of the group may be ('cell group', 'flock group', 'home group', etc.), any home fellowship is meant to help its members towards spiritual growth (Mt 28:19; Jn 21:15–17; Ac 20:28)

The home fellowship is to help Christians learn of Christ, and to encourage them towards holy living

Being part of a home group is not so much going to meetings, but rather entering into meaningful relationships with fellow-Christians

Home fellowships were of key importance for the dynamic growth of the Early Church (Ac 2:46; 12:12; 16:40; Col 4:15; Phm 2)

B. Before starting a home fellowship

1. A leader must be selected
2. He must be trained as to how to lead such a fellowship
3. One must prayerfully choose those who are to join the group

4. The potential participants must be taught some basic principles:
   — they need to understand the goals (Col 1:28–29; 2 Ti 2:2)
   — they need to recognise the authority of the group leader
   — they need to be committed to him and the other group members

C. According to Ac 2:42, there are four main activities

1. Learning together, through biblical teaching received (Ac 20:20)
   — it must be practically related to everyday living (Mk 12:41–44)
   — it must lead to **knowledge** as well as to **action** (Jas 1:22)
   — possible learning areas: effective prayer; spiritual leadership in the family; the use of the tongue; responsible handling of money; keeping the Sabbath; worldliness/holiness; etc.
2. Fellowshipping with one another
   — sharing (victories: for encouragement; needs: for prayer)
   — caring (Gal 6:2)
   — worshipping (Eph 5:19)
   — socialising
3. Breaking bread together
4. Praying with and for one another (Ac 12:12)

D. Some practical advice for the home fellowship leader

Prepare the meetings diligently (above all through prayer)

Make everyone feel welcome
Lead, but do not dominate the conversation
(Suggest ideas, refer back to Scripture, clarify, sum up)
Stimulate the shy to participate as well
(Encourage, ask helpful questions)
Keep loving control over those who might digress, distract, etc.
Do not allow the meetings to develop into a monotonous routine
Periodically, invite unbelievers that they might be introduced to Christ
When your group grows to over fifteen, divide it up and form a second one
Train a co-leader who will be able either to take over this new group or replace you (then you take the new group)
Seek to integrate your home group into the life of the local church

E. How everyone ought to participate

Be open to God: He wants to use your gifts as a blessing to the others
Be open before the others: sincerely share your life with them
Be humble: prefer one another
Be committed: remain faithful and loyal

For further consideration:

Which principles are exemplified in the life-style of the early Christians (Ac 2:42–47; 4:32–35)?

(27)

Commitment to the Great Commission

A. The utmost importance of mission work

1. God has always desired to see all peoples of the earth blessed (Gen 12:2–3; Ps 67:1–3; Isa 66:19–20; 1 Ti 2:3–4; Rev 7:9–11)
2. God made His only Son a missionary (Jn 3:16)
3. God gave the power of the Holy Spirit for the work of world missions (Ac 1:8)
4. God has left His church on earth so that through mission work, it will function as an occupational army in enemy territory (2 Co 4:3–4)
5. Mission work brings blessings on the missionary, the church, the world
6. The fulfilling of the Great Commission will determine the time of Christ's return and the end of the world (Mt 24:14)

B. What does the Great Commission imply?

It means that Jesus Christ has commissioned all those who follow Him as true disciples, to spread the gospel amongst all the peoples on earth:
— we have been sent (Jn 20:21; 2 Co 5:20)
— we have been sent as the Lord Jesus' witnesses (Ac 1:8)
— we have been sent into all the world (Mt 28:19)
— we have been sent to every individual (Mk 16:15)
— we have been sent to preach the gospel (Mk 16:15)

102

— we have been sent to train all people groups in discipleship (Mt 28:19)
— we have been sent to minister in the power of the Spirit (Ac 1:8)

C. It starts right on our doorstep

The Great Commission sends us into all the world, but that world begins right at home. Therefore:
— we are to testify to our relatives, neighbours, and friends
— we are to witness at our place of work (school, factory, office, etc.)
— if God calls us to another village, city or country to spread the gospel there, we must be obedient to His call

D. How can we play a practical part in fulfilling the Great Commission?

1. Through our praying
   For instance, we can pray for:
   — open doors for the gospel   (Col 4:3)
   — protection for the missionaries   (Ro 15:30–31)
   — boldness and power in preaching   (Ac 4:29–31)
   — more workers to be sent into the harvest   (Mt 9:38)
2. Through our giving
   We can give money (see 2 Co 8:1–4), but – more importantly – we can offer ourselves/our children for missionary service
3. Through our going
   A hunter does not wait for the game to come to him, he goes to it. So we must **go** into all the world to reach the unreached with the message of God's love in Christ

E. Why every true disciple must be involved in fulfilling the Great Commission

1. God has sent every disciple to go and tell the world of His love
   (Mk 16:15; Jn 3:16)
2. If we do not go, we become guilty before God and man
   (Pr 24:11–12)
3. The value of one soul is greater than all the world's riches
   (Mt 16:26)
4. Mankind is in desperate need
   (Think of hunger, fear, guilt, hopelessness, Satanic bondages, etc.)
5. Those who never hear the gospel will be eternally lost
   (Ro 10:14; Jn 3:18)
6. More than half of the world population has never heard the gospel

Do we love God enough to commit ourselves wholeheartedly to His desire to see all the world reached?

For further consideration:

How do you understand 1 Co 15:34 and 2 Pe 3:11–12 in the light of the Great Commission?

(28)

How to Lead Someone to Christ

A. Necessary pre-conditions

Make sure that you are adequately prepared
(love, Scripture knowledge, techniques of approach,
etc.)
Pray that God will lead you to the very person whose
heart He has already prepared
Win the confidence of that person by building up a
relationship with him (friendship evangelism)
Rely on the Holy Spirit for guidance and wisdom

B. How to direct the conversation

1. Share the gospel message
   — God loved the world (Jn 3:16)
   — but all men have sinned (Ro 3:23)
   — sin brings about spiritual death (Ro 6:23)
   — God gave Jesus who died for the sins of mankind (Isa 53:5–6)
   — Christ rose from the dead and is able to save (1 Co 15:4; Heb 7:25)
   — in order to be forgiven, a sinner must take two steps:
      turning from all his sinful ways: repentance (Ac 3:19)
      believing in Jesus: saving faith (Jn 1:12)
2. Let him count the cost
   — Lk 14:25–33; 9:57–62
   — Emphasise that receiving Jesus also means to make Him totally Lord of one's life (Ac 2:36)

     — He must be willing to confess Christ publicly (Ro 10:9–10)

     — He must be willing to forsake all idols (e.g. ancestral worship)

3. Explain to him his utmost need of Christ (Jn 3:18, 36; Ac 4:12)

4. See if the Holy Spirit has brought about genuine conviction of sin (Jn 16:8)

5. Challenge him to repent and to put his trust in Jesus (see pages 36–8)

6. Ask him to pray aloud the sinner's prayer:

'O Jesus, I realise that I am a sinner, and I am sorry for my sins. Thank you that you died for me on the cross. Please forgive me my sins. I turn from and forsake all my sinful ways. I ask you into my life as my Lord and Saviour. Thank you for the new life you are giving me now. Amen'

7. Explain to him the basis of assurance of salvation (see page 39)

8. Point out to him the practice of confession and forgiveness (1 Jn 1:9)

C. Help him to get started in his new walk as a Christian

Pray for him every day

Give him some good Christian literature to study

Introduce him to an alive Christian fellowship or church

If at all possible, meet with him regularly to disciple him

Encourage him towards personal growth in Christ through:

     — daily prayer   (Lk 18:1)

     — daily reading of the Word   (Ac 17:11)

- trusting in Jesus (Jn 6:28–29)
- obedience (Ac 5:32)
- having fellowship with other born-
  again believers (Ac 2:42)
- witnessing (Lk 8:39)
- working for God (Jn 9:4)

D. Blessings of soul-winning

Souls are being saved from perdition (Jn 3:16)
It causes joy in heaven (Lk 15:5–7, 22–24)
Jesus is being rewarded for His suffering (Isa 53:11)
It brings joy to the soul-winner (Php 4:1)

For further consideration:

Compare the different approaches Jesus took in Jn
3:1–21 and Jn 4:1–42

(29)

How to Disciple Others (Part 1)

A. As true followers of Jesus, we are expected to make disciples

Mt 28:19; 2 Ti 2:2
When we have reached maturity in Christ (or at least progressed considerably towards it), we are expected to transfer our life in Christ to other Christians, so that they are led to maturity and multiplication (see pages 23 and 24)

B. Securing an effective approach

There are three main avenues to discipleship training:
1. the big group   (Mt 5:1–2)
2. the small group   (Mt 13:36–52; Jn 13:1–20)
3. one-to-one training   (Mt 17:25–27; Jn 21:15–22)
This last method is the most effective
— you can more easily develop a deeper relationship (friendship)
— you can focus on the individual needs and questions of that particular disciple
— you can be more flexible in arranging times to be spent together
The ideal approach is the combination of all three methods
— that is the way which Jesus chose for training the Twelve

— if possible, attend with the disciple the same church (big group), and the same home fellowship (small group), and then add individual discipling (one-to-one)

C. How to identify who to disciple

1. Pray for wisdom to disciple the right people (See Jesus' example in Lk 6:12–13)
2. Keep your eyes open
The potential disciple may be among those belonging to your church, youth group or home fellowship; he may be a relative, friend, fellow-student, a colleague at work, etc.
3. Aim at a high standard
It seems that the efficiency of discipleship training depends on the extent to which potential disciples fulfil the five basic preconditions mentioned earlier (see page 27)
4. Establish the discipleship-relationship
— be willing to take the initiative and invite someone into a discipleship-relationship
— state your twofold goal of maturity and multiplication
— explain clearly what kind of commitment you expect (e.g.: how much time you would spend with him each week; ask him if, according to Heb 13:17, he is willing to submit to your spiritual leadership during the training process)
— ask the potential disciple to pray as to whether God confirms to him to commit himself also to this intensive discipleship training

D. Some warnings

Do not commit yourself to anybody whom God has not shown you clearly (God has not promised His help or blessing for any steps that we take outside of His will)

Do not take on more disciples than you can responsibly handle

Because of the close relationship, the high level of openness, and the sometimes intimate aspects to be considered (e.g. the thought life), one should rather not disciple anybody of the opposite sex

Do not 'compete' with your pastor; on the contrary, co-operate with the church leadership in the discipling of its members

For further consideration:

What can we gather from the apostle Paul's selection of disciples, as in the cases of Silas (Ac 15:22, 32, 40) and Timothy (Ac 16:1–3; 2 Ti 2:2)?

(30)

How to Disciple Others (Part 2)

A. Organising a one-to-one discipleship training session

It is important to come together regularly
- meet at least for one hour every week
- choose a place where you will be undisturbed
- as the discipler, you must plan the meeting carefully

How to proceed during the session:

Step 1: Open with a short prayer
Ask for the guidance of the Holy Spirit, and pray for a fruitful time together

Step 2: Share on your experiences during the past week
- your openness will encourage the disciple to be open too
- share on victories as well as defeats
- check on the assignment you gave the week before (see below)
- be open for questions/problems brought up by the disciple (But: Do not spend all your time sorting out problems; instead, plan in advance to give not more than 20 minutes, for instance, to Step 2)

Step 3: Give instruction
- make the study of God's Word the priority
- open the Scriptures to the disciple so that he can learn biblical principles (see Jesus' example in Lk 24:45)
- follow a specific plan to cover the basic areas of discipleship training (e.g. start with treating the subjects introduced in this handbook)
- give the disciple an assignment for the following

week (e.g.: to read three chapters in a book on prayer; to write down his testimony; to study Abraham as an example of faith)

Step 4: Close with joint prayer
— praise God together; thank Him for the time you just had; intercede for various needs; etc.
— do not neglect to pray for one another during the week!

B. Building up the disciple

The disciple must be taught on three levels:
1. **knowledge** through your instruction
   (e.g.: he receives teaching on principles of guidance)
2. **skills** through practical experience with you
   (e.g.: you show him how to give a testimony)
3. **new convictions** through transformation
   (e.g.: he becomes convinced that it is indispensable to get up early enough to ensure a beneficial quiet time)

Some hints for motivating the disciple towards growth:
— be a challenging example through your life-style
— communicate joy and enthusiasm as a Christian and discipler
— encourage him
  (Show interest; mention the potential you see in him; express your appreciation of him)
— give him faith challenges
— hand more and more responsibility over to him
  (e.g.: let him first pray, then teach, finally lead in your home group)
— pray for him
— show him unconditional love
— be readily available to him
  Highly important: As a true friend, share your life

with him. Spend as much time with him as possible beyond the bare minimum of one hour a week

For further consideration:

As you read Mk 2–6, which principles become manifest in the way in which Jesus chose and trained His twelve disciples?

(31)

The Urgency of the Kingdom

A. God desires to see His Kingdom established

This perspective was a central theme in the Lord Jesus' preaching and teaching (see e.g.: Mt 4:17; 4:23; 6:33; 9:35; 13:1–52; Ac 1:3)
The Lord Jesus lived and died for this goal (Col 1:13)
It is mentioned as a specific request in the Lord's Prayer (Mt 6:10)

B. All history focuses in the establishing of the Kingdom of God

The Kingdom of God among men begins with God's rule in the human heart (Lk 17:21; Ro 14:17)
The world will first be evangelised, then the end will come (Mt 24:14)
Jesus will return as King of kings (1 Th 4:16; Rev 17:14)
We must be ready for that great day (Mt 24:37–44; 2 Pe 3:10)
The full manifestation of the Kingdom will be in eternity (2 Pe 3:13)
All true Christians will be part of that eternal Kingdom (Mt 26:29)

C. Reasons for the urgency of the Kingdom

1. The unsatisfied longings of the Father-heart of God (Jer 3:19; 13:11)
2. The love of God (Jn 3:16)
3. The compassion of God (Mt 9:36; Lk 13:34)
4. Jesus has not yet seen the full reward of His suffering (Isa 53:10–12)
   — He paid the highest price (1 Pe 1:18–19)
   — He paid it in order for all men to be saved (1 Ti 2:3–4)
5. The utmost value of each human soul (Mk 8:36)
6. The threat of the devil to the souls of men (1 Pe 5:8)
7. The torment of the unredeemed
   — on earth: lack of peace/joy/hope/forgiveness/fulfilment
   — for eternity: suffering permanent separation from God's love
8. The impending doom for all unbelievers
   — God's wrath rests over them (Jn 3:36)
   — the certainty of divine judgement (Gal 6:7; Heb 9:27)
9. The command of the Great Commission
   — it puts every Christian under absolute obligation
   — its scope is universal
      all nations are to be reached (Mt 28:19)
      . every individual is to be reached (Mk 16:15)
   — as Christians, we carry responsibility for lost souls (Pr 24:11–12; Eze 33:8–9)

D. Some biblical personalities that show this urgency

The Lord Jesus
   — Lk 4:43
   — Jn 10:16
   — Jn 9:4

The apostle Peter
  — 2 Pe 1:5–11
  — 2 Pe 3:11, 14, 17–18
  — 2 Pe 3:12
The apostle Paul
  — Ac 20:24
  — Eph 5:16
  — Php 3:12–14

E. This urgency should be part of every true disciple's world perspective

Our commitment to see the Kingdom established must be:

determined	(Lk 9:62, see also Isa 50:7)
wise	(Eph 5:15)
wholehearted	(Jer 48:10)
zealous	(Mt 11:12; 2 Pe 3:12)

For further consideration:

Reflect upon the apostle Paul's statements in Php 2:12 and Eph 5:14–18

Appendix

(a)

Abbreviations for the Books of the Bible

A. Old Testament

Ge	Genesis	SS	Song of Solomon
Ex	Exodus	Isa	Isaiah
Lev	Leviticus	Jer	Jeremiah
Nu	Numbers	La	Lamentations
Dt	Deuteronomy	Eze	Ezekiel
Jos	Joshua	Da	Daniel
Jdg	Judges	Hos	Hosea
Ru	Ruth	Joel	Joel
Sa	1 and 2 Samuel	Am	Amos
Ki	1 and 2 Kings	Ob	Obadiah
Ch	1 and 2 Chronicles	Jnh	Jonah
Ezr	Ezra	Mic	Micah
Ne	Nehemiah	Na	Nahum
Est	Esther	Hab	Habakkuk
Job	Job	Zep	Zephaniah
Ps	Psalms	Hag	Haggai
Pr	Proverbs	Zec	Zechariah
Ecc	Ecclesiastes	Mal	Malachi

B. New Testament

		Ro	Romans
Mt	Matthew	Co	1 and 2 Corinthians
Mk	Mark	Gal	Galatians
Lk	Luke	Eph	Ephesians
Jn	John	Php	Philippians
Ac	Acts	Col	Colossians

Th	1 and 2 Thessalonians	Jas	James
Ti	1 and 2 Timothy	Pe	1 and 2 Peter
Tit	Titus	Jn	1, 2 and 3 John
Phm	Philemon	Jude	Jude
Heb	Hebrews	Rev	Revelation

(b)

A Bible Reading Plan for a Year

This calendar divides the Holy Scriptures into 365 portions requiring only about ten to fifteen minutes daily for one to read the entire Bible through in one year.

Date	JANUARY		FEBRUARY		MARCH	
1.	Genesis	1–3	Leviticus	1–4	Deuteronomy	8–10
2.		4–6		5–7		11–13
3.		7–10		8–10		14–16
4.		11–13		11–13:28		17–20
5.		14–17		13:29–14		21–23
6.		18–20		15–17		24–27
7.		21–23		18–20		28
8.		24–25		21–23		29–31
9.		26–28		24–25		32–34
10.		29–30		26–27	Joshua	1–4
11.		31–33	Numbers	1–2		5–7
12.		34–36		3		8–9
13.		37–39		4–5		10–12
14.		40–41		6–7		13–15
15.		42–44		8–10		16–18
16.		45–47		11–13		19–21
17.		48–50		14–15		22–24
18.	Exodus	1–3		16–18	Judges	1–3
19.		4–6		19–21		4–6
20.		7–9		22–23		7–8
21.		10–12		24–26		9–10
22.		13–15		27–29		11–13
23.		16–18		30–31		14–17
24.		19–21		32–33		18–19
25.		22–24		34–36		20–21
26.		25–27	Deuteronomy	1–2	Ruth	
27.		28–29		3–4	1 Samuel	1–3
28.		30–32		5–7		4–6
29.		33–35		–		7–9
30.		36–38		–		10–12
31.		39–40		–		13–14

	APRIL		MAY		JUNE
Date					
1.	1 Samuel	15–16	2 Kings	11–13	Ezra	9–10
2.		17–18		14–16	Nehemiah	1–4
3.	.	19–21		17–18		5–7
4.		22–24		19–21		8–9
5.		25–27		22–23		10–11
6.		28–31		24–25		12–13
7.	2 Samuel	1–3	1 Chronicles	1–3	Esther	1–3
8.		4–7		4–5		4–7
9.		8–10		6–7		8–10
10.		11–12		8–10	Job	1–5
11.		13–14		11–13		6–10
12.		15–17		14–16		11–15
13.		18–19		17–20		16–20
14.		20–22		21–23		21–26
15.		23–24		24–26		27–30
16.	1 Kings	1–2:34		27–29		31–34
17.		2:35–5	2 Chronicles	1–4		35–38
18.		6–7		5–7		39–42
19.		8		8–11	Psalms	1–9
20.		9–10		12–15		10–18
21.		11–12		16–19		19–25
22.		13–14		20–22		26–33
23.		15–16		23–25		34–37
24.		17–18		26–28		38–44
25.		19–20		29–30		45–51
26.		21–22		31–32		52–60
27.	2 Kings	1–3		33–34		61–68
28.		4–5		35–36		69–73
29.		6–8	Ezra	1–3		74–78
30.		9–10		4–6		79–86
31.		–		7–8		–

	JULY		AUGUST		SEPTEMBER	
Date						
1.	Psalms	87–91	Isaiah	46–49	Ezekiel	17–19
2.		92–101		50–53		20–21
3.		102–105		54–58		22–23
4.		106–109		59–62		24–26
5.		110–118		63–66		27–29
6.		119	Jeremiah	1–3		30–32
7.		120–134		4–6		33–35
8.		135–141		7–9		36–38
9.		142–150		10–12		39–40
10.	Proverbs	1–5		13–15		41–43
11.		6–10		16–18		44–45
12.		11–14		19–22		46–48
13.		15–18		23–25	Daniel	1–2
14.		19–22		26–28		3–4
15.		23–27		29–30		5–6
16.		28–31		31–32		7–9
17.	Ecclesiastes	1–4		33–35		10–12
18.		5–8		36–38	Hosea	1–7
19.	Ec. 9–Song	2		39–41		8–14
20.	Song of Sol.	3–8		42–44	Joel	
21.	Isaiah	1–4		45–48	Amos	1–5
22.		5–8		49–50		6–9
23.		9–12		51	Obadiah–Jonah	
24.		13–16		52	Micah	1–5
25.		17–22	Lamentations	1–2	Micah 6–Nahum	
26.		23–27		3–5	Hab.–Zeph.	1
27.		28–30	Ezekiel	1–3	Zeph. 2–Haggai	
28.		31–35		4–7	Zechariah	1–7
29.		36–38		8–11		8–13
30.		39–42		12–14	Zech. 14–Malachi	
31.		43–45		15–16		–

Date	OCTOBER		NOVEMBER		DECEMBER	
1.	Matthew	1–4	Luke	23–24	1 Corinthians	12–14
2.		5–6	John	1–3		15–16
3.		7–9		4–5	2 Corinthians	1–4
4.		10–11		6–7		5–9
5.		12–13		8–9		10–13
6.		14–15		10–11	Galatians	1–3
7.		16–18		12–13		4–6
8.		19–21		14–16	Ephesians	1–3
9.		22–23		17–18		4–6
10.		24–25		19–21	Philippians	
11.		26	Acts	1–2	Colossians	
12.		27–28		3–5	1 Thessalonians	
13.	Mark	1–3		6–7	2 Thessalonians	
14.		4–5		8–9	1 Timothy	
15.		6–7		10–12	2 Timothy	
16.		8–9		13–14	Titus–Philemon	
17.		10–11		15–16	Hebrews	1–5
18.		12–14:25		17–19		6–9
19.		14:26–16		20–21		10–11
20.	Luke	1		22–23		12–13
21.		2–3		24–26	James	
22.		4–5		27–28	1 Peter	
23.		6–7	Romans	1–3	2 Peter	
24.		8		4–7	1 John	
25.		9–10		8–9	2 Jn., 3 Jn., Jude	
26.		11–12		10–13	Revelation	1–4
27.		13–14		14–16		5–8
28.		15–16	1 Corinthians	1–4		9–12
29.		17–18		5–8		13–16
30.		19–20		9–11		17–19
31.		21–22		–		20–22

William Caldwell

Used by kind permission of Emmanuel Press, White River, R.S.A.

(c)

Principles for Effective Intercession
by Joy Dawson

1. **Praise God for who He is, and for the privilege of engaging in the same wonderful ministry as the Lord Jesus.**

   Heb 7:25 'He ever lives to make intercession for them [His own],'

   Praise God for the privilege of co-operating with Him in the affairs of men through prayer.

2. **Make sure your heart is clean before God, by having given the Holy Spirit time to convict, should there be any unconfessed sin.**

   Ps 66:18 'If I regard iniquity in my heart, the Lord will not hear me.'

   Ps 139:23–24 'Search me, O God, and know my heart: try me, and know my thoughts: and see if there be any wicked way in me, and lead me in the way everlasting.'

   Check carefully in relation to resentment to anyone.

   Notice the link between forgiveness and prayer in God's Word. When Jesus instructs the disciples how to pay He says, 'Forgive us our debts, as we also have forgiven our debtors' (Mt 6:12), and IMMEDIATELY FOLLOWING the 'Lord's Prayer' He Says, 'For if you forgive men their trespasses, your heavenly Father also will forgive you; but if you do not forgive men their trespasses, neither will your Father forgive your trespasses' (Mt 6:14).

   Again in *Mk 11:25*, 'And whenever you stand

praying, forgive, if you have anything against any-one; so that your Father also who is in heaven may forgive you your trespasses.'

Now notice the link between forgiveness and faith when we pray:

Mk 11:24 'Whatever you ask in prayer, believe that you receive it, and you will.'

Then comes verse 25, warning us to forgive any-one who has wronged us.

Lk 17:3–5 '"Take heed to yourselves; if your brother sins, rebuke him, and if he repents, forgive him; and if he sins against you seven times in the day, and turns to you seven times, and says, 'I repent,' you must forgive him." The apostles said to the Lord, "INCREASE OUR FAITH!" and the Lord said, "If you had faith as a grain of mustard seed, you could say to this sycamine tree, 'Be rooted up, and be planted in the sea,' and it would obey you."'

Job had to forgive his friends for their wrong judging of him, before he could pray effectively for them.

Job 42:10 'And the Lord restored the fortunes of Job, when he prayed for his friends; and the Lord gave Job twice as much as he had before.'

Gal 5:6 'Faith works through love.'

3. **Acknowledge you can't really pray without the direction and energy of the Holy Spirit.**

Ro 8:26 'The Spirit helps us in our weakness; for we do not know how to pray as we ought.'

Ask God to utterly control you by His Spirit, receive by faith that He does, and thank Him.

Eph 5:18 'Be filled with the Spirit.'

Heb 11:6 'Without faith it is impossible to please Him.

125

4. **Deal aggressively with the enemy. Come against him in the all-powerful Name of the Lord Jesus Christ and with the 'sword of the Spirit' – the Word of God.**

   Ja 4:7 'Submit yourselves therefore to God. Resist the devil and he will flee from you.'

5. **Die to your own imaginations, desires, and burdens for what you feel you should pray.**

   Pr 3:5 'Lean not unto your own understanding.'
   Pr 28:26 'He who trusts in his own mind is a fool.'
   Isa 55:8 'My thoughts are not your thoughts.'

6. **Praise God now in faith for the remarkable prayer meeting you're going to have. He's a remarkable God and will do something consistent with His character.**

7. **Wait before God in silent expectancy listening for his direction.**

   Pr 62:5 'For God alone my soul waits in silence, for my hope is from Him.'
   Mic 7:7 'But as for me, I will look to the Lord, I will wait for the God of my salvation; my God will hear me.'
   Ps 81:11–13 'But my people did not listen to my voice; Israel would have none of me. So I gave them over to their stubborn hearts, to follow their own counsels. O that my people would listen to me, that Israel would walk in my ways!'

8. **In obedience and faith, utter what God brings to your mind, believing.**

   Jn 10:27 'My sheep hear my voice . . . and they follow me.'
   Keep asking God for direction, expecting Him to give it to you. He will.

Ps 32:8 'I will instruct you and teach you the way you should go; I will counsel you with my eye upon you.'

Make sure you don't move on to the next subject until you've given God time to discharge all He wants to say to you regarding this particular burden; especially when praying in a group.

Be encouraged from the lives of Moses, Daniel, Paul, and Anna, that God gives revelation to those who make intercession a way of life.

9. **If possible have your Bible with you should God want to give you direction or confirmation from it.**

    Ps 119:105 'Thy word is a lamp to my feet and a light to my path.'

10. **When God ceases to bring things to your mind to pray for, finish by praising and thanking Him for what He has done, reminding yourself of Romans 11:36, 'For from Him and through Him and to Him are all things. To Him be the glory for ever. Amen.'**

A Warning

God knows the weakness of the human heart towards pride, and if we speak of what God has revealed and done in intercession, it may lead to committing this sin.

God shares His secrets with those who are able to keep them.

There may come a time when He definitely prompts us to share, but unless this happens we should remain silent.

Lk 9:36 'And they kept silence and told no one in those days anything of what they had seen.'

Lk 2:19 'But Mary kept all these things, and pondered them in her heart.'